What's inside?

And lots more

For Shannon

Published by Books for little ones Ltd, 416 Harrow rd, London W9 2HX, England

Printed by CreateSpace.com, a member of the Amazon group of companies

ISBN-13: 978-1466496699

Drawing on your computer with Paint:
Colours, Lines, Circles and Rectangles

By G G Watson

Contents

Introduction

Paint is a simple, easy to use drawing program that comes with all PCs running Windows. It's perfect for having fun drawing and colouring on your computer at a very basic level while at the same time learning.

The tools in Paint make it easy to create simple drawings to share with family or friends. My simple drawing exercises are designed to get you drawing even cooler stuff, so let's get going.

Getting Started

To open Paint

If you're using Windows Vista or 7, you can search for Paint on the start menu

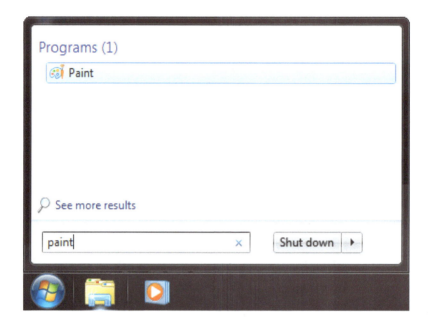

If you're using Win9x to XP, Click Start – All Programs/Programs – Accessories – Paint

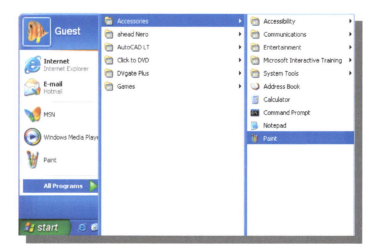

The Paint Screen

The Screen on Windows 7

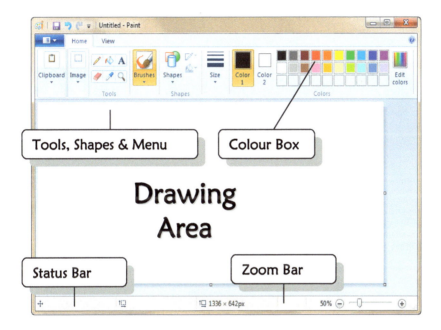

Tools, Shapes & Menu

Colour Box

Drawing Area

Status Bar

Zoom Bar

The Screen on Win9x to XP

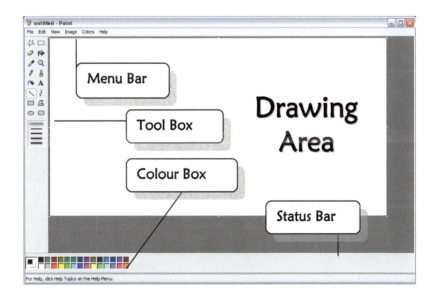

Menu Bar

Tool Box

Drawing Area

Colour Box

Status Bar

Just Colour

Let's do some colouring! The aim here is simple, colour the drawing area with the colours below one at a time. If your favourite colour is not there then do that one too.

Tool

You will need the Fill with Colour tool

Blue

Orange

Green

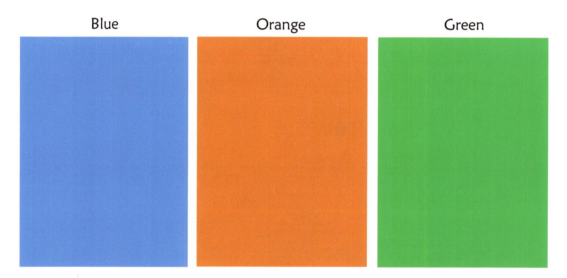

Purple

Yellow

Red

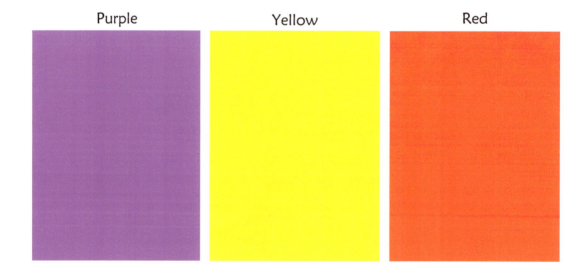

Gold

Black

Pink

Gary

Brown

Lime

Tip
The Drawing Area is Blue.

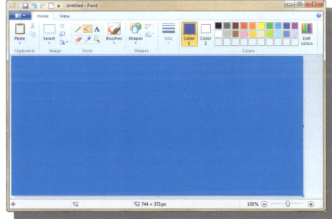

Just Lines

Let's draw lines! The aim here is to draw lines as straight as you can and not too wriggly.

Tool

You will need the Line tool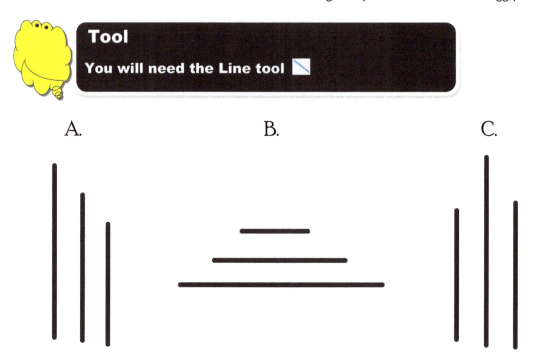

A.   B.   C.

Now draw the same lines in the colour Red. You can also have a go at trying other colours: Blue, Orange and Green.

A.   B.   C.

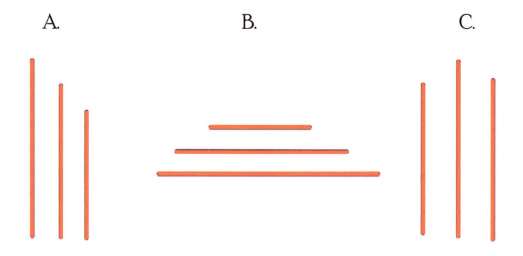

Draw lines to make shapes. Do you know any of these shapes?

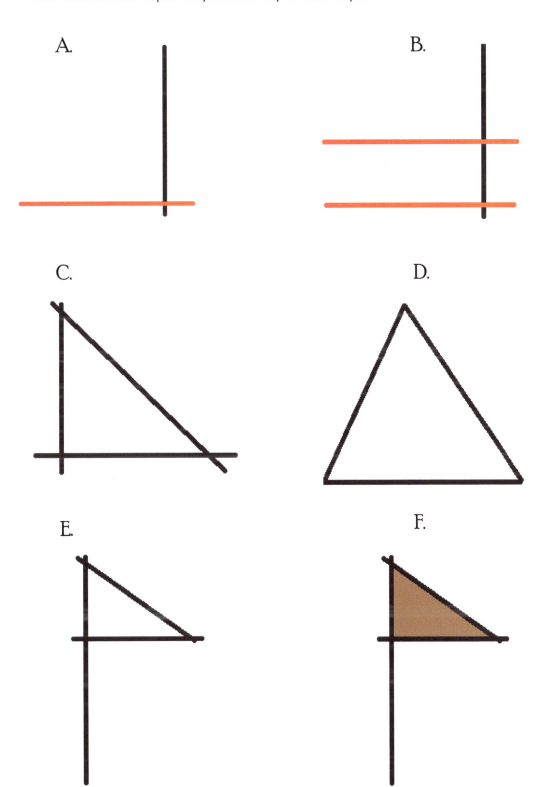

A.

B.

C.

D.

E.

F.

G.

H.

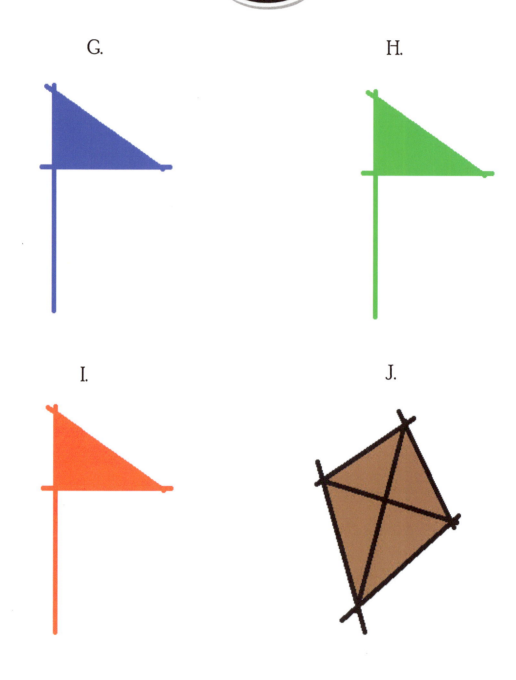

I.

J.

Finally, have a go at drawing this tic tac toe.

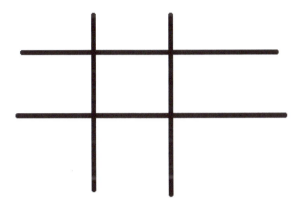

Tips
You can play a game of tic tac toe with someone by using the Pencil tool
Made a mistake? Just Undo or Edit-Undo and start again!

Tiptro Step by Step Help

Draw a red line in 3 steps.

Paint on Windows 7

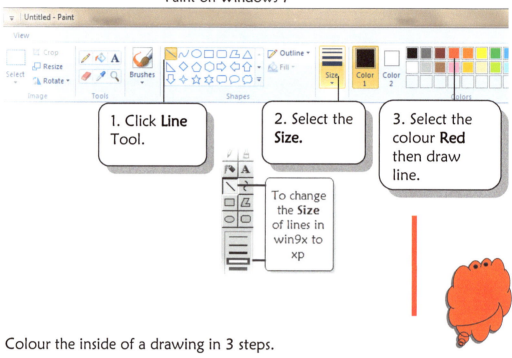

1. Click **Line** Tool.

2. Select the **Size.**

3. Select the colour **Red** then draw line.

To change the **Size** of lines in win9x to xp

Colour the inside of a drawing in 3 steps.

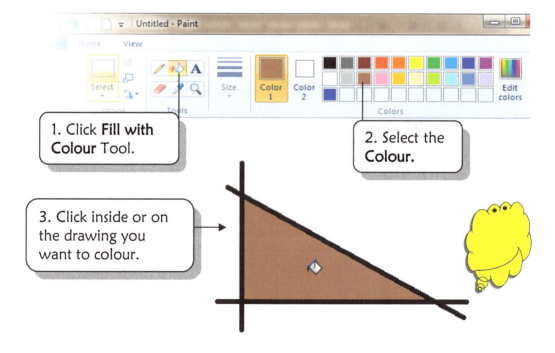

1. Click **Fill with Colour** Tool.

2. Select the **Colour.**

3. Click inside or on the drawing you want to colour.

Just Circles

Oh just what a can we draw with circles? Lots of things! The aim here is to draw circles. They don't have to be perfect, just as close as you can to what's below.

Draw and colour the circles below. Use whatever colour you want!

Tool

You will need the Oval/Circle tool ⬭

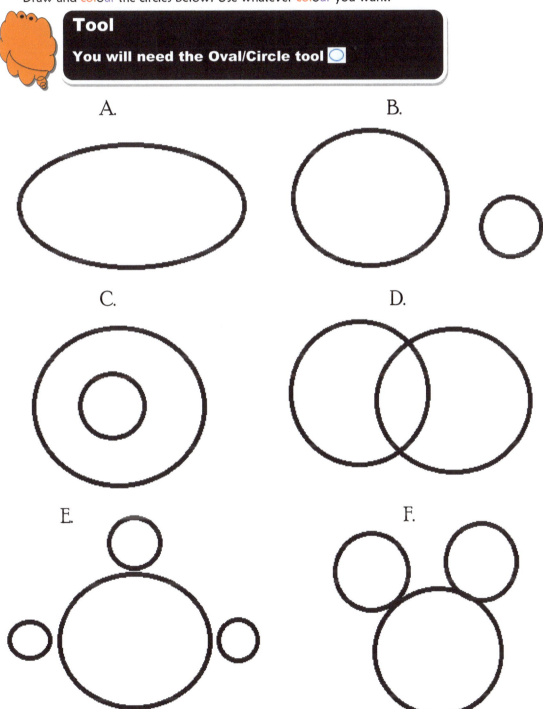

A.

B.

C.

D.

E.

F.

Now draw these drawings below. Don't be afraid to give them your own style and colour.

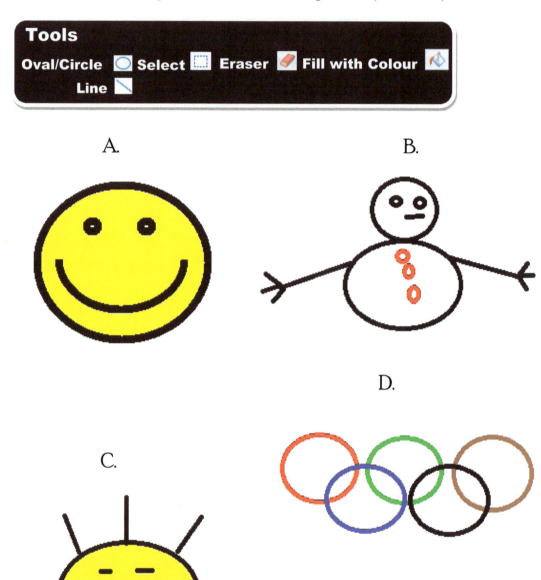

Tools

Oval/Circle ◯ Select ☐ Eraser 🧹 Fill with Colour 🪣
Line ◣

A.

B.

C.

D.

E.

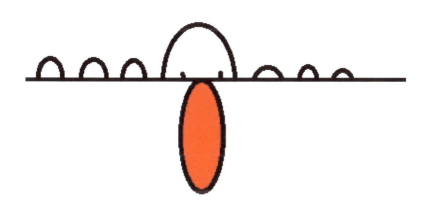

F.

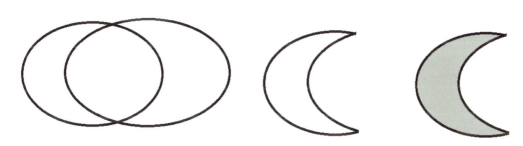

Tip
Need help with tools? See *How to use the Paint tools in this book* on page 20.

Just Rectangles

There are lots of things that have a rectangle or square shape, stuff we use and see every day like books and TVs. The aim here is to have fun drawing and colouring shapes made with rectangles.

Draw and colour the rectangles below. Use whatever colour you want!

Tool

You will need the Rectangle tool ☐

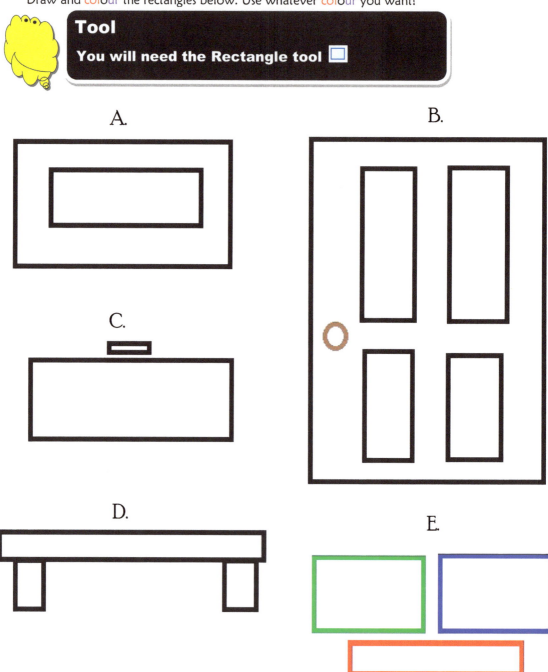

A.

B.

C.

D.

E.

F.

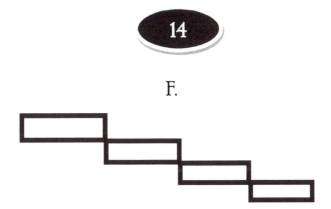

Now draw the drawings below. Don't be afraid to give them your own style and colour.

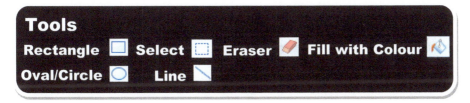

A.

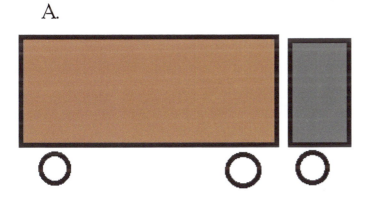

B.

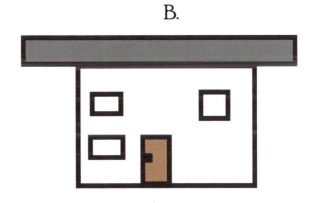

C.

D.

E.

F.

Bagel

Draw a bagel in two easy steps. Have fun drawing by adding your own bits, changing colours, shapes whatever!

Step 1 | Draw two circles.

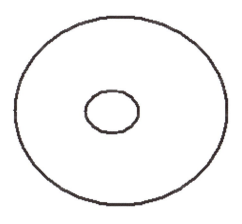

Step 2 |
Colour the inside as shown then use the

Brush tool  or
to insert some raisins.

Brushes

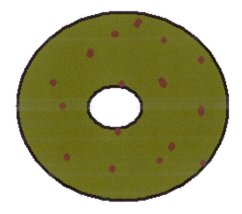

Reminder
It's ok if your drawing looks a bit different from the ones on this page.

TRY THIS

A.

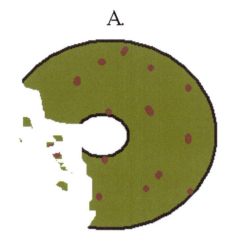

B.

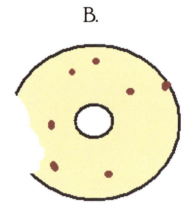

Tip

Use the Free-Form Select tool or to create similar effects as shown above.

Teacup

Draw a teacup in two easy steps.

Step 1 | Draw a circle then draw another circle inside it. Delete a portion as shown by using the Select tool

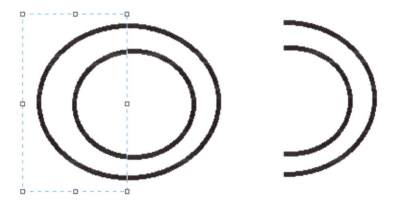

Step 2 | Draw a rectangle then position the remaining portion of the circles as shown using the

Select tool

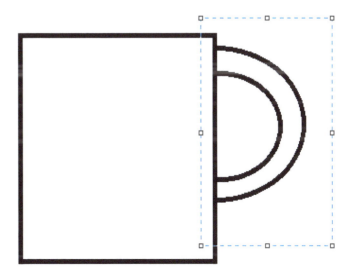

TRY THIS

A.

Type 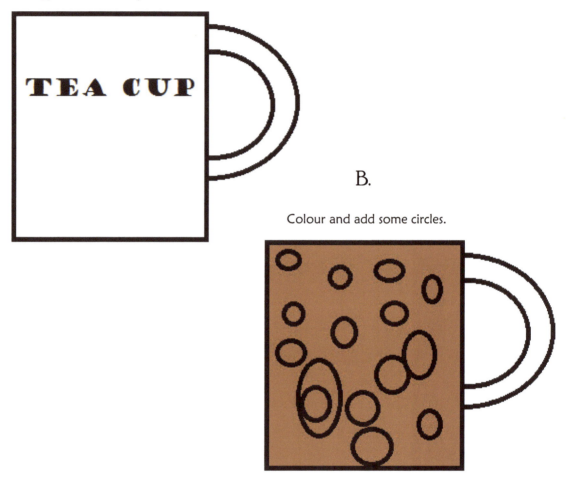 "Tea Cup" in the centre.

B.

Colour and add some circles.

Tips
To type text, click on the Text tool in the toolbox then click and drag on the drawing area.
To move a drawing, select it then click on the drawing and drag.

Castle

Draw and colour a castle in two easy steps.

Step 1

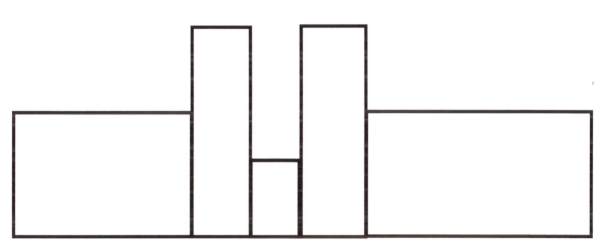

Step 2

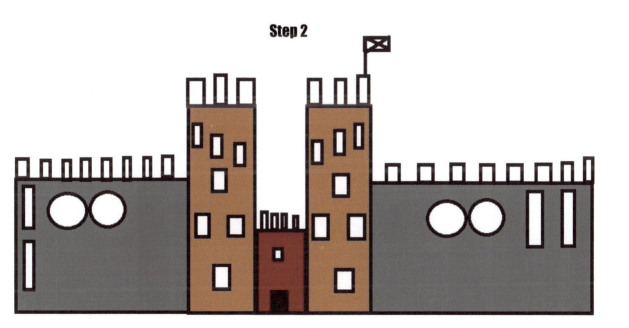

TRY THIS

Clock

Draw and colour a clock in two easy steps.

Step 1 | Draw a circle then a rectangle and then add lines as shown.

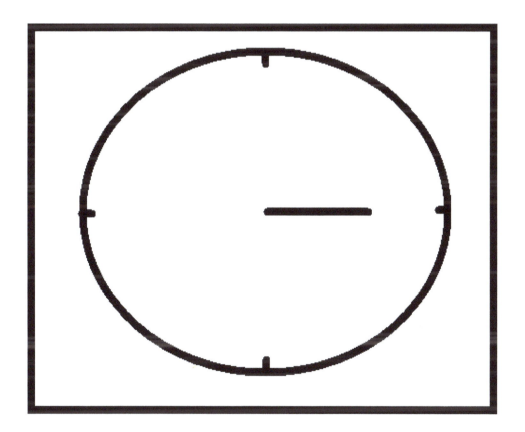

Step 2

Tips

Draw numbers then position them using the Select tool.
Remember to change the line size for the hour, minute & second clock hands.

Pizza

Draw and colour a pizza in two easy steps.

Step 1

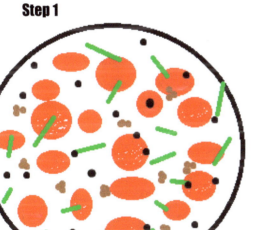

Step 2

Reminder

It's ok if your drawing looks a bit different from the ones on this page.

TRY THIS

PIZZA

Tip
Use the Fill With Colour tool to change colour.

Rainbow

Draw and colour a rainbow in three easy steps.

Step 1

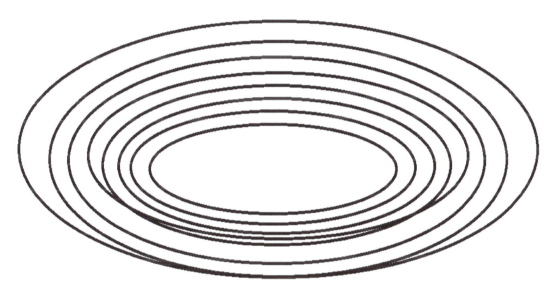

Step 2 | Add colours: Red, Orange, Yellow, Green, Blue, Indigo & Violet.

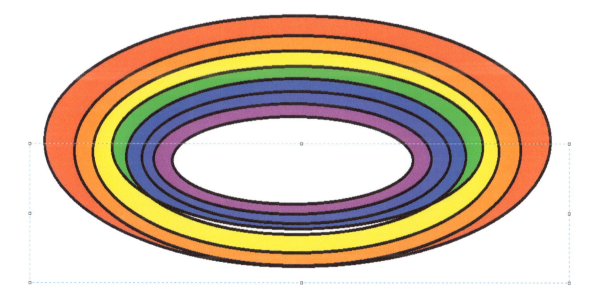

Step 3

TRY THIS

How to use the Paint tools in this book

The Free-Form Select Tool

Selecting the Circle

This tool is used to select and edit drawings that cannot be selected by the Select Tool. When used to select a drawing you can: Move, Cut, Copy, Delete, Flip/Rotate etc. To use, click Free-Form Select then circle the drawing (click & drag) you want to select.

The Select Tool

Selecting the Circle

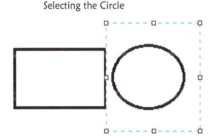

This tool is used to select and edit drawings. When used to select a drawing you can: Move, Cut, Copy, Delete, Flip/Rotate etc. To use, click Free-Form Select then circle the drawing (click & drag) you want to select.

The Transparent image/Selection button

Circle & Rectangle are visible

Use this button to allow drawings to be visible when moving drawings over other drawings. In the example the Circle was drawn, then selected with Select tool, then moved to the position shown on the rectangle.

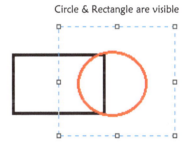

The Opaque image button

Circle in-front and drawing behind is part hidden

Use this button to hide drawing when you move drawing over other drawings. In the example the Circle was drawn, then selected with Select tool, then moved, to the position shown on the rectangle.

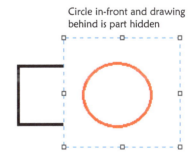

The Oval/Ellipse/Circle Tool

Use this tool to draw circles of all shapes and sizes. To use, just click on the Oval tool, then click and drag on the drawing area.

The Line Tool

This tool is used to draw lines. You can select different line widths or sizes before drawing a line, rectangle, circle or any shape from the sub menu. To use, click Line tool Then click and drag on the drawing area.

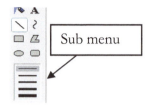

Sub menu

The Rectangle Tool

This tool is used to draw rectangles. To use To use, just click on the Rectangle tool, then click and drag on the drawing area.

The Eraser/Colour Eraser Tool

This tool is used to "rub out" drawings. To use, click on Eraser/Colour Eraser, then click and drag to access the drawing to erase.

The Fill with Colour Tool

This tool is used simply to colour drawings or the entire drawing area. To use this tool, click Fill With colour, click on a desired colour in the colour box then point and click inside the drawing to fill with that colour.

The Magnifier Tool

This tool is used to view a drawing up closer, by making it bigger. To use, click on the Magnify tool then click the area on the object you want to magnify.

The Pencil Tool

This tool is used as a freeform drawing tool. To use, click on the Pencil tool then click & drag on the drawing area.

The Text Tool

This tool is used to add letters, numbers & symbols to the drawing area. To use, click on the Text tool, then click on the drawing area to start typing.

The Brush Tool

Brushes

This tool is used to   add dots to your drawing to give various effects. To use Click on the Brush tool, select brush type then click to apply brush effect.